How To Generate Leads For Your Local Business With Google AdWords Copyright @ 2014 by Kyle Battis and Mike Purvis

Neither the authors nor the publisher assume any responsibility or liability whatsoever on the behalf of the purchaser or reader of these materials.

Any perceived slight of any individual or organization is purely unintentional.

What People Are Saying...

"Kyle and Mike have been responsible for generating <u>hundreds of thousands of dollars</u> for my company!"

-Tellman Knudson

"If it weren't for Kyle and Mike, I am sure I would be nowhere near as successful as I am today. **In the last year I have <u>DOUBLED</u> my business!** Due to this success my wife has been able to quit her job and stay home and raise our son. Kyle and his team have been instrumental: From helping me with website traffic, list building to ad copy and everything in between."

-Geoff Neupert

"The growth in our business since working with Kyle and his team has been unreal and the work that it brought in has been great – we even had to hire another person to keep up!"

-Dick Arpin

"Kyle Battis is one of the few people I go to for new ideas, strategies, and techniques."

-Brian T. Edmondson

"Kyle Battis and Mike Purvis have helped me close the gap between "Idea" and "Done" more times than I can count. I've relied on them over and over to help me bring my campaigns *together, to help me drive traffic and test the effectiveness of my ads, and discover new opportunities to add revenue streams and strategic partnerships. Kyle and Mike are true masters of nearly every skill involved in online marketing, period, end of story.*

-Josh Burns

"Kyle Battis is one of the smartest marketing minds I know."

-Pat Marcello

Your Free Gift

As a way of saying thanks for your purchase, I'm offering a free gift that's special for our readers.

Marketing your business can be a challenging task. To be a successful business owner increasing the reach of how many people know about you and your business can dramatically improve your success. *That's why we publish* our weekly "Marketing Minute" newsletter.

If you would like to claim your free "Marketing Minute" subscription and access the Marketing Minute archives you can sign up at no cost here: *www.NHStrategicMarketing.com/news*

How To Generate Leads For Your Local Business With Google AdWords

A Primer On How To Use Google's Powerful Advertising Platform To Attract and Convert Clients For Your Local Business...

By Kyle Battis and Mike Purvis

Table of Contents

1. Introduction

The Lifeblood of Business

Leads are the lifeblood of any business. Lead generation is a marketing process to stimulate and capture interest in your products or services with the goal of converting as many leads as possible into new customers.

In working with hundreds of business owners ranging from one man operations to $15 Million Dollar a year businesses, one thing we have learned is that **every business wants more leads.**

Interestingly enough - businesses go about trying to obtain a consistent flow of new leads using one of only a handful of messages:

Some use 'hope' as their marketing strategy (*hoping* the phone will ring with a new customer). Although we of course don't endorse this methodology, don't feel bad if you're in this boat. There are a large percentage of business owners who (despite what they may say), are employing this strategy right now. Sadly, many of these businesses only take action to generate a consistent lead flow once business starts slowing down and the 'newness' of their offer or service starts to dissipate. Unfortunately, this is often way too late in the game to turn the tables.

Other, savvy business owners get in the game much earlier, and position their business for steady growth. These business owners create (yes, that's an important distinction - they **create** it - it doesn't happen on it's own), a **predictable and scalable** lead generation system (*system -* another important word we'll cover in more detail later on). As a result, they have a steady flow of interested prospects coming to them on a regular basis - not by accident, but intentionally and deliberately.

We can tell you that when a business has a predictable lead generation system in place, that they're far more likely to grow as large as they would like, as fast as they would like (or if they prefer, maintain a steady flow of leads so their business thrives and they can enjoy the lifestyle they desire - not everyone wants to build a $100 Million company :)

We have no way of knowing what your situation is, but we can tell you that if your goal is to generate more leads for your business then what we will be presenting to you in this book should be of great interest.

What if you had a constant and steady supply of leads for your business?

How would things be better for your business?

Imagine knowing <u>without a doubt</u> that month in and month out you will have a steady flow of qualified leads calling you or contacting you through your website.

Wouldn't it be great to not have "down months," or at the very least, having less of a down month than your competitors?

Imagine knowing that if you wanted to grow sales in your business that you could turn up the lead flow any time you wished quickly and easily.

Wouldn't those be nice options to have?

Life (and business) is always so much easier when you have more options to choose from...

If you had a steady flow of leads for your business you could choose whom you want to do business with. Further, you could put yourself in a position where you don't "have to" work with just any customer or client.

You can instead work with the ones you relate with best.

When you have a steady flow of leads being generated for your business you can 'rest easy' knowing that your business will keep busy. You can avoid the ebbs and flows that your competitors face because they don't have a predictable system to generate leads. We've seen businesses in many industries outpace their competitors because they discovered how to predictably generate leads for their business.

This can be a real game changer for you and your business...

No matter what your current situation, our goal is to introduce you to the possibilities of harnessing the power of the Internet to generate qualified leads for your business.

Our hope it that you will experience a powerful "Ah-Ha" moment and that we will have introduced you to how you can leverage Internet traffic and funnel qualified website visitors towards you and your business. Without further adieu let's dig in.

2. The Way Your Customers Find You Has Changed

Traditional marketing methods are becoming less effective - period.

No matter what business you are in, the way your customers find you has changed. The "old way" customers found you was through advertising in the Yellow Pages, taking out the occasional newspaper ad, television ads, advertising in magazines, and maybe even sending direct mail to everyone in your city or town.

That was then.

Today's consumers are looking for businesses like yours in a completely different place. **They have moved online to find you.**

Today, buyers can do their own research online and can find a variety of educational resources through search engines, social media, and other online channels.

Today's buyer can learn a great deal about a product or service <u>before</u> ever having to even speak to anyone from your business.

In nature those animals that adapt to changes in their environment are the ones who thrive. The same is true in business. Many a business has gone under because "nothing works anymore."

We beg to differ. The "old" and tired ways of marketing their businesses don't work anymore (or at the very least are less effective). Now, we will be the first one to tell you that we don't believe that any business should ONLY use one way to market themselves. That's foolish.

The smart business owner has a variety of marketing channels in play at the same time to drive a steady flow of leads their way. The point we're making here is that the environment for *how* customers find you has evolved and thus businesses must make sure that they build their digital presence *as well as* their offline presence.

Lead Generation Defined

Lead generation is a marketing process to stimulate and capture interest in your products or services with the goal of converting as many leads as possible into new customers.

Put another way, it is the creation of consumer interest or inquiry into your products or services. In an ideal world, more of the right people should know about your business today than yesterday. Mature business owners realize that this is a <u>deliberate process</u>.

It's not based in "hoping" the phone rings or "hoping" that business picks up. Lead Generation is a mindset and something that should happen regularly and consistently. Business expert Dan Kennedy teaches that it's an activity that every business owner should take action on every single day – without fail.

Getting the phone to ring or having qualified leads contact you via your website is not likely to happen <u>without doing some activity</u> to generate interest.

Generating interest and awareness is just the first step in the process; getting that prospect to take action and visit your site is the next. From there you have to have a good 'reason why' they should contact you. We'll talk more about how to convert leads more effectively later in this book.

A Range of Options To Generate Leads But One Champion Comes Out On Top For Online Lead Generation

The methods for generating leads typically fall under a wide variety of offline marketing, online marketing, free methods, and paid methods.

On the next page, you'll find a short list (far from exhaustive) but this will give you an idea where Google AdWords fits in the lead generation range.

Lead Generation Channels (The Short List)

	Offline	Online
Paid	• Direct mail • TV ads • Radio Ads • Newspaper Ads • Yellow Pages	• Google AdWords (our favorite and #1 method and the focus of this book) • Facebook Ads • Banner Ads
Free	• Referrals / Word of Mouth • Free Publicity • Networking • Public Speaking	• Online Reviews on Google, Yelp, etc. • Social Media marketing (Facebook Fan Page, Twitter, Pintrest, etc.)

There are pluses and minuses to every approach. While this book is about paid Lead Generation with Google AdWords, we highly recommend having as many different lead sources as possible. Of course, out of all of the online options available, **Google AdWords is our champion method.**

We'll go over Google AdWords thoroughly in this book and make a case for why it is one of our favorite methods but for now, we'd like to share a little story from our friend **Todd Brown**, an expert marketer and creator of the "Marketing Funnel Automation" system.

Todd's Brown's Story of "How This Business Advice Has Been a Game Changer" and What It Has To Do With Google AdWords Lead Generation For Your Business

Todd Brown is a master marketer and recently shared this story:

A few years ago I moved my family down to South Florida. I was tired of the cold New Jersey winters.

And I was ready for some palm trees and year-round gorgeous weather. A couple months after moving I became friends with Rich Schefren (the Founder of Strategic Profits). I later ran the marketing for Strategic Profits for a handful of years.

Well, very early before I was a partner at Strategic Profits, I had a meeting with Rich at a Starbucks cafe in Barnes and Noble in Boca Raton to talk about some of the struggles I was having growing my main company at the time.

And, it was at that meeting that Rich shared with me one single piece of advice that forever changed my business and income. To say it's been a game-changer is really an understatement.

Here's the gist of what he said:

"Until you can pay for the acquisition of customers, you do not have a real business. All you have is a promotion."

What Rich was saying was this... Until you are using paid traffic (media buying) to acquire new customers, you will continue to have ups and downs in lead flow, ups and downs in sales, ups and downs in income, and limited scalability (growth potential).

You see... reliance on social media, search engine optimization, product launches, strategic partnerships, and/or affiliates makes your business vulnerable.

*Vulnerable... because... SEO Algorithms change. Partners and affiliates flake-out. And you have little if any REAL control. Whereas, once you understand even the basics of buying media... paid traffic... (both Offline and Online) **the game immediately changes for you**.*

With paid traffic you have full control over what happens, when, where, and how with your website traffic.

Your lead flow becomes steady, sales become consistent, and your income becomes dependable (assuming you have a good offer, of course). Fact is: With media buying done correctly, getting traffic to your site is never, ever a problem. "

-Courtesy of Todd Brown,
Marketing Funnel Automation

No matter what business you are in, generating inbound leads is a great thing some businesses just use them in different ways. How the leads are handled depends on what type of business you are in, what your sales process is, and a lot of other factors.

Let's move on.

3. Three Specific Ways Businesses Can Generate Leads

1. **Drive Inquiry Phone Calls and Appointment Requests.** This may be to claim a free (or paid), consultation or meeting; a trial of your product or service; a free analysis, quote etc. - anything that may lead to doing business with you in the very near future. Typically these calls or requests (through contact forms on your website), act as a 'small commitment' on your prospects behalf, that gives you a chance to get in front of them and present your case for why your business, is the only choice. These prospects are well qualified when done correctly, so that your only conversing with leads that are most likely to turn into cash for your business. This is one of the most common forms of lead generation that most small businesses gravitate towards and can be very effective.

2. **Offer an Online or Offline Newsletter.** Newsletters work very well in a wide variety of businesses. The goal is to deliver interesting content along with your sales messages, and eventually convert that prospect into a customer by delivering value and building the relationship.

3. **Utilize Multi-Step Sales Funnels.** We regularly work with businesses that use advanced CRM (Customer Relationship Management) software and a very advanced, multi-step marketing strategy. These systems may use a combination of online and offline capture and followup points.

If your business isn't generating the leads it should be - this will help...

We can't be sure of your current situation and if you are in fact already generating enough leads for your business, but we can make an educated guess that you would like to see <u>more</u> leads (and higher quality leads), coming in every week.

No matter if your business is struggling due to lack of leads or, if you would just like to ramp up your current lead generation efforts, Google holds a lot of potential to help your business grow.

<u>Imagine if</u>, within just a couple of days, you could establish a steady flow of qualified leads from the Internet...

Its more than possible and we'll show you how...

You're about to discover our favorite way to grow a local business in a scalable and predictable manner, and that my friend is with paid advertising - specifically the with Google AdWords advertising platform.

Google™ AdWords

Google AdWords is an incredible opportunity for rapid growth and profits, and is an advertising platform unlike anything ever created to help small businesses like yours market their business.

If you are ready to join the ranks of small business owners who are successfully generating leads online and growing their bottom line, let this be your primer on the subject to get you pointed in the right direction.

We are exited to have this opportunity to reach out to small business owners like you that are looking to dominate the Internet and grow their business. We've been marketing online since 1999 and have been investing in paid Google Advertising for a very long time.

We've managed campaigns that were investing $75,000/month in Google Advertising as well as small campaigns of just $10 a day. We've seen the amazing potential this platform can deliver, and we're excited for you!

It's an exciting time for you as a business owner right now as there are more people searching for local businesses like yours than ever before. Its been reported that **97% of today's consumers will use a search engine like Google to start their search for a local business.**

Some Interesting Google AdWords Trivia To Illustrate The Potential That You Are About To Tap Into...

- Date of Google AdWords launch was October 23, 2000
- There are 12.477 Billion searches every month!
- 97% of Google's revenue comes from advertising (aka Google AdWords!)
- The average click-through rate for an ad in the first position is 7.94%!
- For high commercial intent searches, the top 3 ad spots receive about 40% of the clicks on the entire page!
- Businesses make an average of $2 in revenue for every $1 that they spend on AdWords!

Google AdWords gives your business the ability to be at the top of page 1 FAST!

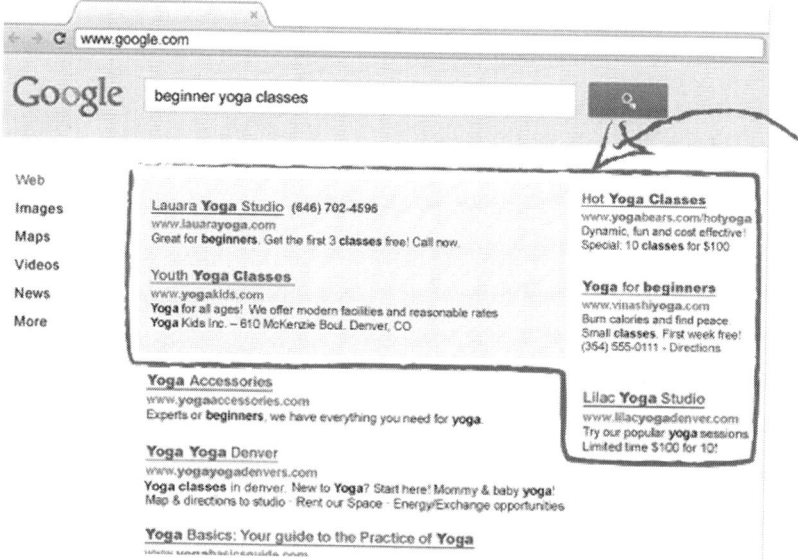

It is our belief, and we invite you to join us in it, that when it comes to marketing your business, everything you do needs to get **real and trackable results.**

We come from an environment where we absolutely needed to know that for every $1 invested in Google AdWords that we were going to make $2 back (or more!) We have successfully started Ad campaigns from scratch that profitably cranked out new leads and customers on the back end and that's what we want to share with you.

Generating a steady flow of leads from the Internet for your business is possible too...

Now, this is a vastly different approach than Madison Avenue ad agencies have brainwashed business owners without multi-million dollar ad budgets to take.

Creating national branding campaigns for a big money brand like *Coca Cola* is one thing, but as a small business owner that doesn't have the same kind of resources; you need to be sure that <u>every dollar</u> you invest will grow your business.

Most traditional advertising options don't deliver the potential results that Google AdWords can.

There are a lot of factors that go into getting solid results with AdWords, but the tips and strategies we will be detailing here are a great first step to seeing solid, measurable growth in your business.

4. Why Google AdWords Is Superior To Traditional Advertising Methods

The times are changing - there's just no denying it. Actually, I suppose a better way to frame it would be: "The times have changed!"

In the good old days you could simply advertise in the Yellow Pages, in the local newspaper every once in a while; and you would be all set for advertising your business and ensuring leads would be coming your way.

As the Internet has matured, the Yellow Pages have been dying a slow death and circulation of newspapers has been waning as people get their news from other sources.

In today's digital age, your business needs to be *where* your potential customers are searching, *when* they are searching for you...

The Yellow Pages are dead and serve as glorified doorstops for most people...

Television commercials, radio spots, every door direct mailings, newspaper ads, and billboards have traditionally been the go-to routes for gaining exposure and generating leads for local businesses.

That was then...

These methods of advertising are all *"interruption advertising,"* meaning that you are trying to interrupt as many people as possible with your message and hopefully you find a few that are interested.

How To Generate Leads For Your Local Business With Google AdWords

This is why response rates are so low with this type of advertising.

These methods of attracting the attention of potential clients are antiquated, and much less effective when compared to the sniper-like precision of Google AdWords.

You will never find a higher quality lead than someone that:

1. Is in your local area

2. Does a Google search for what your business delivers

3. Sees your ad at the top of the page

4. Clicks on your ad

5. And one minute later calls <u>your</u> business or fills out a contact form.

Someone searching for your type of business on Google is more than likely looking for help or answers from you or one of your competitors. They are searching on Google because they need what you offer *right now.* They are much further along in the buying process then someone that you are trying to prospect with interruption advertising.

This is a really key point so we recommend reading that last sentence again.

Google is a "buying engine" and if you learn how to leverage it effectively you will win...

Anybody that has ever been involved in any type of sales or marketing knows that there is a HUGE difference between these two scenarios:

1. When a potential customer is proactively searching <u>for you</u>, finds you, and calls you

2. You, trying to prospect from the masses of prospects that aren't necessarily interested in what you have to offer, are cold calling or interrupting people with your advertising.

There is simply no comparison in the quality of the lead, and in addition, *advertising on Google is 100% completely measurable so you will know EXACTLY what your return on investment is.*

You would be hard pressed to get the same kind of performance and **clarity** from any other type of advertising that you invest your money in.

Google's Ads Interface Gives You 100% Clarity On What Is Working to Make Your Phone and Your Cash Register Ring...

Fortunately, you have an incredibly powerful tool at your disposal, which takes advantage of beautifully executed timing when delivering ads to people who are **already searching** for your type of business. And it does this while delivering you transparent lead generation results so you can track exactly what you return on investment is. It's called Google AdWords, and it is the greatest thing that ever happened to the online advertising world.

There's a reason Google's stock is over $1,100/ share and it's because Google AdWords is so very effective....

There are many entrepreneurial local business owners that have built multi-million dollar businesses using Google AdWords as their primary means of generating new leads and new business. There really is nothing else like it in the world today. If there was, believe us, we would be using it and suggesting that you do too!

Don't get us wrong...

Google AdWords isn't the only *'tool in our toolbox'* and we don't ever recommend getting all your leads from just one source (*"one is always the worst number in any business"* as Dan Kennedy taught us).

We do run Bing ads, Facebook Ads, and utilize other forms of online and offline marketing but our most powerful tool to make the phone ring and attract qualified leads has been Google AdWords.

We start here BEFORE adding on these other streams of traffic.

Onwards...

5. Generating Leads Online With Google AdWords

Let's start off this section by making an important point.

Google makes its money through AdWords (it's proprietary advertising platform).

They <u>do not</u> make money through organic search engine results. Google wants you to advertise and they want you to get good results so that you keep spending more and more money on advertising year after year.

It's a Win-Win Partnership With Your Business and Google - They will help you get qualified leads in exchange for your advertising dollars...

A lot of local businesses we have worked with over the years have this misconception that, *"no one clicks on the ads that appear at the top of the search results."*

This couldn't be further from the truth.

It's true that a lot of people click on the first or second organically generated result. However, many people don't even know those first three results that appear at the top of the page are ads!

Furthermore, you only need a small percentage of people to click on your ad to have more leads than you can handle. If you believe that no one clicks on ads and aren't willing to make the investment in a strong AdWords campaign, you're cutting yourself off from a HUGE source of predictable, scalable and profitable lead generation.

"But Can't I Just Rank My Website With Search Engine Optimization To Get On the Front Page Of Google?"

As a modern business you're aware that the Internet plays a big role in how customers find you. It stands to reason that showing up on the first page of Google gives your business a better chance to attract new customers. You may be thinking to yourself, *"Why don't I just put all my time and money into SEO and getting my website to rank higher in the search engines?"*

We aren't against SEO at all. The Problem is that a few cute animals may be preventing your business from getting on the front page of Google organically.

Let us explain…

Penguins, Pandas and ***Hummingbirds*** are generally thought of as cute and benign animals right? I am here to warn you that they are ***BUSINESS KILLERS.*** You may wonder, "How could these loveable animals possibly kill my business?"

Penguin, Panda and *Hummingbird* are also names for some of the recent Google Search Algorithm updates that the 'Big G' has made to their search ranking formula.

This formula dictates which businesses show up in its search ranks when people search for a given keyword such as "personal injury attorney," "emergency veterinarian," "antique furniture restoration," or whatever it is your business delivers.

These animal-named search updates have KILLED many a business owner's lead generation **overnight** because that business owner made the mistake of relying on organic rankings for that keyword as the lifeblood of their business.

We aren't against SEO but we are against putting all your stock into Search Engine Optimization as the *only* method to generate leads for your business. We have done our fair share of SEO for clients and it is an incredibly frustrating game because the target keeps moving.

We know many a business owner that has invested tens of thousands of dollars into ranking their websites only to have their site buried in the search results due to a sudden change in the ranking algorithm.

Overnight they lost their first page rankings and their lead flow dried up. Building your business on an unstable foundation isn't a wise move.

While investing effort into ranking organically can work it's a tricky and unpredictable game that we don't put a lot of stock into when it comes to predictably getting more leads from the Internet.

Further,

It takes a LOT of time, money, and effort to organically rank in search results on Google for any valuable keyword. No matter what business you are in, no matter if you are brand new or have been in business for some time, you're probably not going to rank high on search results through SEO without a lot of time and effort.

Our friend and Search Engine Optimization expert Pat Marcello was always fond of telling us that, "SEO is a Marathon, not a sprint." If you do SEO the right way, the way Pat does it, it can be a viable strategy.

Just know that it will take time, will take a large monetary investment, and you may not see results from these efforts for 6-12 months. Lastly, if another algorithm change comes down the pipes and you don't have an expert like Pat running your SEO campaign, you could lose your rankings overnight.

There are no guarantees in SEO and that's why we are such huge advocates of Google AdWords. With AdWords, and the right strategy, you're all but guaranteed to get found on page 1 **from Day 1!**

* * * * * *

The New Future of SEO For Local Businesses? 'Local Search Credibility'

If you're on page 2, 3, 4 or 5 you might just as well be on page 500 in the Google Search results - very few searches happen beyond the 1st page listings (one of our colleagues says, *"if you want to hide a body put it on the 2nd page of Google 'cuz no one will ever find it there!"*).

If people don't find what they're looking for right away, they try another search - rarely do searchers go pages deep in the search results.

We want to make a few points here before we move on – and yes, SEO is important, very important, but there's a really important point few agencies want you to know about - and w'm going to share it with you right here - consider it a 'Bonus Gift' :)

SEO for local businesses is NOT the same as it is for large companies, national (or international), brands, mass-market offers or the likes. SEO for local businesses is (now more than ever), about being the best choice for your local audience – nothing more.

Local SEO comes down to a few simple things in our opinion:

1. Google wants to know that you are who you say you are. It's pretty simple. Google relies on what we call 'citations' to verify you're legit. Essentially, it's nothing more than having your Name, Address, and Phone Number (known to citation experts like us as your 'NAP'), on relevant, socially active and well-established sites. Think Yelp, Trip Advisor or industry specific review sites like ILoveInns.com or the likes (most industries has their own set of highly relevant citation sites). The more complete and consistent your listings are across the web, and the more 'good reputation' citation sites you place on, the better.

2. What your customers are saying about you. The second thing that's critically important for Local Business SEO is your online reputation. This as well is really simple. Google looks to see what the general public thinks of your business (yes the reviews at Yelp, Trip Advisor and very importantly, on your Google+ page, are an important part of 'The New SEO' for local businesses). Basically Search Engines rely on your *past* customers to let them know if you're a good business to send *future* customers to - if the general public has better things to say about your business than your competitors in the same geographic area, then you're placements get extra 'points' in the Local SEO Game.

3. Social Activity Involving Your Business. One other important factor for Local SEO is the conversations you and your customers are having about your business online. The more actively engaged you (and your customers), are on Social Media (yes, Facebook and the likes really do matter for SEO :), the better chance you have at out-ranking your local competition.

If you take a 30k foot view - it's really simple - if you want Organic listings for your local business, forget everything you've heard from SEO Agencies, forums, online blogs etc. and instead focus on sharing great content on your website (via blog) and Word Of Mouth.

We know... it's so last decade right? But you know what else... We firmly believe SEO is finally headed in the right direction, and soon enough it won't even be called SEO anymore - We think of SEO for local business today as something else entirely – let's call it *'Local Search Credibility'*. Instead of trying to manipulate the search engines with cleverly modified content, meta this and backlink that - all you *really* need to do is:

1. Tell the right sites who you are, where you're located, and how you can be reached - and be meticulously consistent. We actually have a very affordable, one time service for this called 'Local Visibility' – if you're interested, call us and we can outline it for you in about 5 minutes - we don't use smoke and mirrors to justify high prices - all we focus on is results. and...

2. Run a business worth saying good things about (which you're probably already doing anyway), and then give your patrons a way to let the *right* online places know what a great experience they had. This is important - you have to have a system for actively asking for positive feedback, and then directing people to the right places to leave it. If you don't have a system to do this, please contact us and we can help. It's very simply one of the best investments you can make in establishing a stellar online reputation. and finally...

3. Keep a conversation going with your customers online - in the right places and in the right way. Again, this isn't difficult. You just need a system for that (and we can help with this as well).

Now, this report has nothing to do with SEO, but we wanted to clear the air a bit first, dispel some of the common misconceptions about what it means to be 'ranking on page 1' and to also be clear: SEO *is* important - and much easier than most agencies will have you believe (local businesses have a distinct advantage in this way), and it's something we recommend you *do* work on in your business - but it's not the most important thing.

Our customers that take a multi-channel approach to their marketing efforts always make more money, plain and simple, but in our opinion, SEO falls second to the number 1 type of traffic we recommend - and that my friend, is Search Advertising on the Google AdWords Platform.

In our opinion, for local business owners, there is no faster, more immediate, trackable, scalable and predictable way to grow your business using the internet.

So now that we have that out of the way, let's talk about the good stuff, and how you can start driving new leads for your business (almost overnight - yes, really!)

* * * * * *

Ok, so back to the SEO versus AdWords point...

If that business had taken that same money and invested it into Google AdWords, they would have received new leads and clients from Day 1...

No 6-12 month ramp up period needed.

In turn, this means they would barely have come out of pocket, because they could have turned a profit in the first month and then just reinvested those profits.

Let me ask you...

Would you rather pay $1,000 per month for a year just to "possibly" get on page one for your desired keyword - knowing that if Google changes their SEO algorithm again you could lose it all overnight without any warning?!

Or, would you prefer to **instantly** be at the top of the search results for hundreds of different keyword variations (not just a couple of keywords like with SEO), having new leads and new clients coming in your door right away?

This is also where we love working on Google AdWords more than any other form of advertising media. When you think back to what we said about TV, radio, newspapers, the Yellow Pages, and some other advertising methods, the point we want to convey is just how expensive those formats are.

You can spend thousands of dollars and still not know how well your ad is working for a very long time.

With AdWords, you can run a simple test campaign for about a week, spend only a few hundred dollars, and see <u>instant results</u>.

When that one week test is done, you'll have a ton of data telling you what keywords worked, how many clicks you got, how many leads came in, and how many new signed clients you have retained for the money invested.

From there you can refine your AdWords campaign even further by continuing to split-test ads and deciding how much you want to expand your campaign.

For example if you spend $1,000 and you make back $5,000, the next month you may very well want to spend $5,000 and make back $25,000.

Its simple math really.

6. How To Predictably Get More New Customers

This is almost too simple really - but here it is:

The best way to get more new customers is by showing up in front of them right when they need you most...

One of the biggest problems we hear over and over from new clients is that they <u>don't</u> have a predictable system for growth and new client acquisition in their business.

If the phone isn't ringing as much as you would like and you don't have a *PREDICTABLE SYSTEM* in place to magnetically attract new customers to you; then what you are about to read will help you immensely.

In this section we will present 3 ways to use Google AdWords to grow your business.

And remember… a whopping **97% of consumers** use the Internet to find answers to questions they need and business to give their hard-earned money to.

Let's dig in.

3 Ways To Use Google AdWords to Grow Your Business

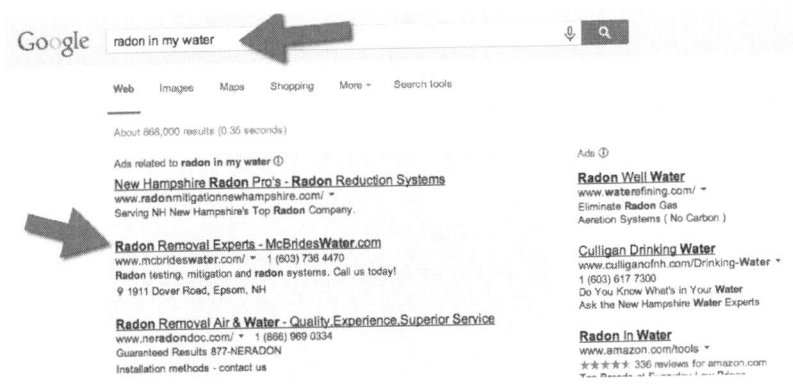

1. Show up WHEN and WHERE they are looking for you

– As mentioned above, 97% of today's consumers go to the Internet to find answers to their questions or problems, to find help, and to research whom to do business with. The fine folks at Google have termed this behavior the "Google Zero moment of Truth."

Above is a screenshot of a Google search we did for *"Radon in my water"* while we were at my Concord, NH home.

Notice we didn't put NH anywhere in the Google search bar, but notice the second listing is from our Client Bill McBride of *McBrides Water.* Google knows where we are searching from so they show us Bill's ad that he is using to target potential customers in a certain area he selected.

Bill only gets charged when an interested prospect clicks on his ad (hence the 'Pay Per Click' name). Bill and his team have been successfully leveraging Google AdWords and showing up in front of potential customers WHEN and WHERE they are looking for answers to their questions. *Smart and VERY effective.*

<u>Exercise</u>: Do some Google Searches for key terms that potential customers might search for to find YOUR business. Who is showing up in the Ad blocks on the front page of Google? Are your competitors there? How much are you losing by not showing up there?

2. Mobile Advertising is <u>HUGE</u>! - There are 6.8 billion people on the planet and 5.1 billion own a cell phone (but only 4.2 billion own a toothbrush - yikes)! HALF of all searches done on a Mobile Phone are people looking for local businesses like yours.

70% of all mobile searches result in action within 1 hour for a local business. Mobile is HUGE and will only be more important in the coming years so getting Mobile Ads that can show up to potential customers when they're searching for you on their Mobile phones is CRITICAL! The nice thing with these ads is that you can have a "Click To Call" button IN the ad (which makes it super EASY for targeted customers to call your business!).

3. Get <u>Added Leverage</u> When Someone Visits Your Website from ANY Traffic Source

Retargeting (also known as remarketing), is a form of online advertising that can help you keep your brand in front of 'bounced' traffic <u>after they leave your website</u>.

For most websites, only 2% of web traffic converts on the first visit. Retargeting is a tool designed to help companies reach the 98% of users who *don't* convert right away.

Retargeting is so effective because it focuses your advertising spend on **people who are already familiar with your brand and have recently demonstrated interest.** That's why most business owners who use it see a higher ROI than from most other digital channels.

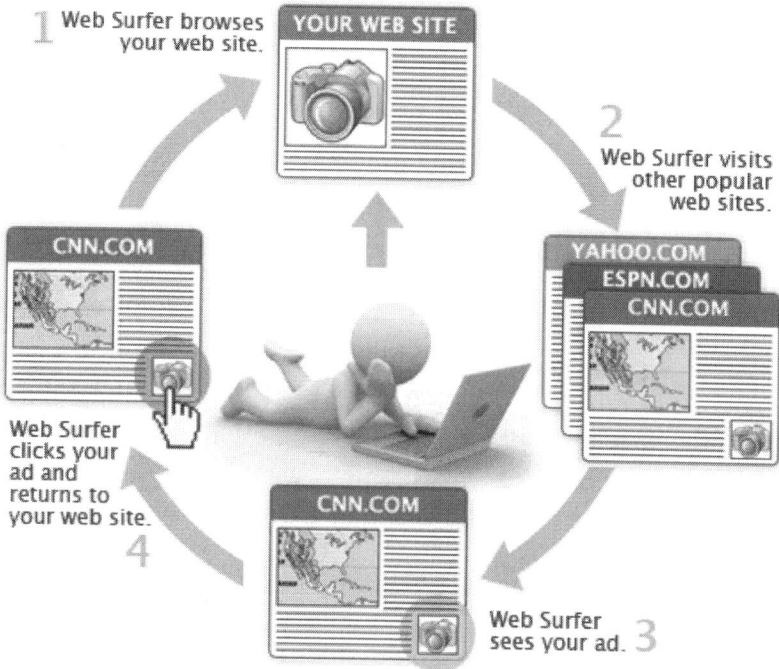

Here is an interesting factoid to drive home the power of Remarketing with Google AdWords: *Yankee*

Candles reports that Remarketing allowed increased conversion rates by 600% while cutting cost per conversion by 50%

If you want to see serious results that are reliable and measurable, you have to be using AdWords. In the next section, I'll go over how you can implement an effective AdWords campaign, or if you are already running one, how you can make it perform even better.

7. Strategies to Improve Your AdWords Conversion

Ok, before we get into some of the more tactical stuff, how about a little bonus...

1 Sneaky Trick To Immediately Beat Out Your AdWords Competition

Your Company - www.yourwebsite.com
Your Address and Phone Number

Google loves local businesses and they give you a huge advantage when advertising on their platform (that most of your competitors likely don't know about).

First, Google lets you integrate your Google Plus Local account with your AdWords account. This means when people from your local area are searching, your ad will be MUCH bigger than other ads with your phone number and address right there in the ad!

It maybe an old adage but in the world of Internet Marketing, size does matter. If the ad is bigger, people are going to see it first; if the ad is well formatted they're going to read the details, and you know what they're going to probably do next? They're going to click on it (or call the phone number in the ad)!

Because you're local, your location information is going to appear in the ad (when you integrate your Google Plus account). You're going to see an increase in business!

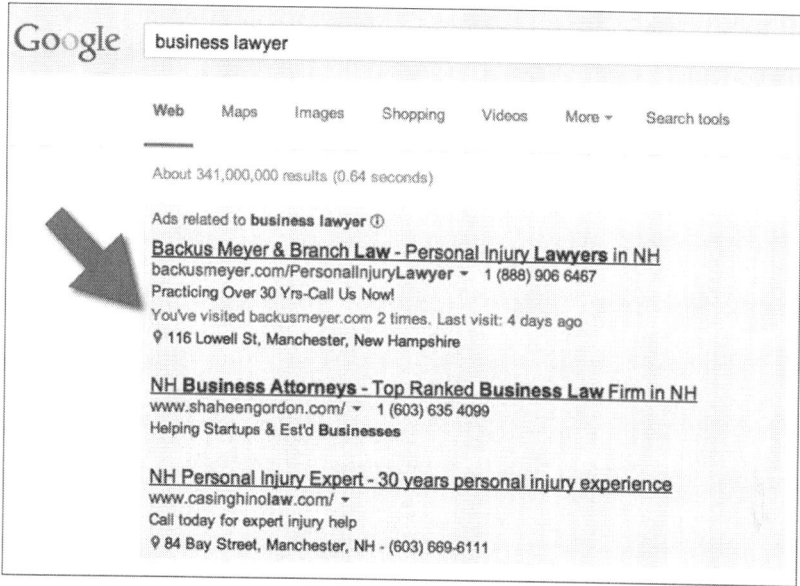

Example of a Google + Enhanced Ad for a Local Business - Notice How big it is

And what's even better, when you link your Google Plus Local account with your Google Adwords Campaign, and you've acquired a star rating - your customer feedback will even show in the ad - *and* your phone number is displayed as well. All of this extra 'presence' gives you a huge boost in click through rate - and ultimately, in conversion!

Ok, that was fun, right?

So hopefully, at this point, you're completely on board and ready to give your AdWords campaign the attention and care it deserves. If so, then there are some things we feel you should be trying - and some bad habits we want to help you avoid - so let's talk about those.

How To Optimize Your Google AdWords Lead Generation System

The difference between a Google AdWords campaign that "didn't work" and one that *is* generating a predictable flow of profitable leads comes down to some surprisingly small distinctions.

They say, "Small hinges swing BIG doors." If you truly want to get leads from the Internet, then these tips we're about to share are crucial to your success. This section may be a little over your head if you've never seen the inside of an AdWords account, but we think it's important you know that these are practices that SHOULD be happening in a properly run Google AdWords account for your local business.

Here is the first big tip to optimize your campaigns...

Always **be split testing <u>multiple</u> ads for increased Click Through Rate (CTR), and Conversions**

Getting people to click on your ads is only the first step. You might be getting some clicks, you might be seeing some incoming business, but that doesn't mean you couldn't be doing better!

Consistent and creative split testing is an absolute essential to the health of your campaign.

Here's a cool illustration that shows how Split Testing works:

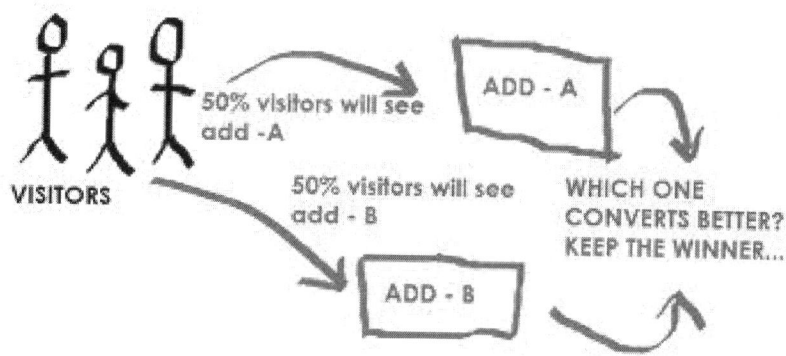

A Google AdWords Essential – Split Testing Your Ads Yields Better Results Over Time

Split test *multiple* ads to find the ones that get you the highest click through rate (CTR) - it's simple. And don't stop after just one test - you should *always* be trying to beat your control (the current winner).

When it comes to your ads - good is never good enough (if you want to make more money anyway :)

Most businesses that try to do Google AdWords on their own <u>FAIL</u> because they don't have a high converting landing page (more on that soon) and/or they have not split tested multiple ads to increase their click through rate.

Google will actually reward you for having a well-built AdWords campaign that is getting lots of clicks!

If your ad is generating a lot of clicks that are going to your business and generating leads (hence conversions), Google is going to give you a <u>cheaper cost-per-click</u>... rewarding you for having great ads that are getting lots of clicks and providing a good experience for their users (as reflected in the high conversion rate).

The higher the clickthrough rate of your ad - the cheaper you get clicks for.

Google is actually helping you generate more business, and saving you money on your clicks. Yes, they actually *reward* 'good advertisers'.

Constant Split Testing allows you to determine what is working, why it's working, and then scale the elements that are bringing you success across your entire PPC campaign. And keep in mind - in this context, we're discussing ads in your account - but you should also always be testing elements on your landing page, in your site, ways you answer the phone etc. We could go on for a good long time on what to test, but to keep is simple... test everything (and win!).

As crazy as it sounds, sometimes the difference between a great campaign and a doomed campaign can be one word in the ad, or the position of a form on the landing page, or the wrong color headline - it could be just one little thing.

But you'll never know if you don't test.

And test again.

And, continue testing.

Unlike direct mail and direct marketing methods, online testing is cheap and often provides you with near instant results so you can react quickly and build more intelligent ad campaigns that elevate your income.

A trained Google AdWords expert will <u>always</u> be split testing your Ads to ensure your campaign continues to improve and deliver more leads for a lower cost.

Ok, how about another important tip? Here's a big one:

Drive Your Traffic To A High-Converting Landing Page – NOT The Home Page Of Your Website...

When someone clicks on your ad, where are you going to drop that visitor?

You might be thinking that you've spent a ton of money, time, and energy building a slick looking, informative website that's the perfect place to send your traffic and draw in some clients.

We understand that you may believe this is a reasonable idea, but it could actually cost you a lot of money if you were to do that.

Believe it or not, you're far more likely to **lose clients** if you're routing all your ad traffic to your main website!

We see this mistake all the time in many campaigns.

For Example, we did a search today and found this ad running in Google when searching for an Attorney. *(**Note** – we blurred out the website name so if he sees this he won't feel so bad that we were picking on him).* ;-)

Here is the ad:

NH Appeals Lawyer - ▓▓▓▓▓▓▓▓▓
▓▓▓▓▓▓▓ ▾
Handling civil & criminal appeals. Free consultation. Call us today.

Note, the ad isn't actually all that bad and we're sure it gets clicked, but remember the 'click' is only part of the equation to successfully pulling in qualified leads.

Where the ad drives is less than ideal and our bet is that this advertiser is spending a LOT of money for very expensive legal traffic. As an aside, did you know that Attorney related clicks are one of the four most expensive clicks money can buy? So if you're paying for this campaign, then you want to make sure you're converting as many of those clicks into customers as possible - and driving them to your homepage isn't going to cut it!

This specific ad drove to a page that was missing a phone number or even a simple web form (there was no immediate way for the visitor to contact the attorney!), *and* even beyond that - there was no clear compelling offer - a huge set of mistakes!

You want to ensure that WHERE you are driving that visitor is optimized to convert them into a real lead.

Don't make them think...

Don't make them hunt around your website looking for your phone number or contact form.

Make it intuitive and easy for a visitor to know what they need to do to get what they were promised in the ad.

It may seem like an obvious concept but you would be AMAZED at how many advertisers and business owners mix this one up! And now you're probably thinking... "So where exactly should I send these visits then?"

We think you'll like this next bit ;)

What Millions of Dollars In Google Pay Per Click Advertising Has Shown Is The <u>BEST</u> Place To Send Your Visitors To Convert More Leads...

Our team has invested millions of dollars in advertising revenue and we can tell you this from our years of testing: **you <u>MUST</u> send AdWords traffic to a landing page.**

It needs to be a simple, one page, easy to read landing page that invites the prospect to **take action now.**

This can be a hidden landing page on your website (i.e. www.YourWebsite.com/landing-page-1) or it can be on a completely different website (www.YourWebsite.*net*) dedicated only to your paid traffic driving efforts.

These landing pages get the person that clicked on your ad involved right away and contacting you <u>before they get distracted</u>.

If your traffic is being sent to your main website, you run a constant risk of that visitor never taking action. They did not pick up the phone. They did not fill out a contact form. You just lost a potential client and wasted the ad revenue you spent to get them to click on your ad.

High-converting landing pages are specifically designed using a proven template to get your prospects to do one of two things...

1. Pick up the phone and call you!

2. Fill out a Contact Form

Your slick, expensive looking main website is not enough to draw in new clients to your business. A landing page is essential for getting those people looking to retain your services to pick up the phone and actually schedule an appointment.

Here are a couple Landing page examples we found after a quick search to show you what a professionally designed landing page 'may' look like.

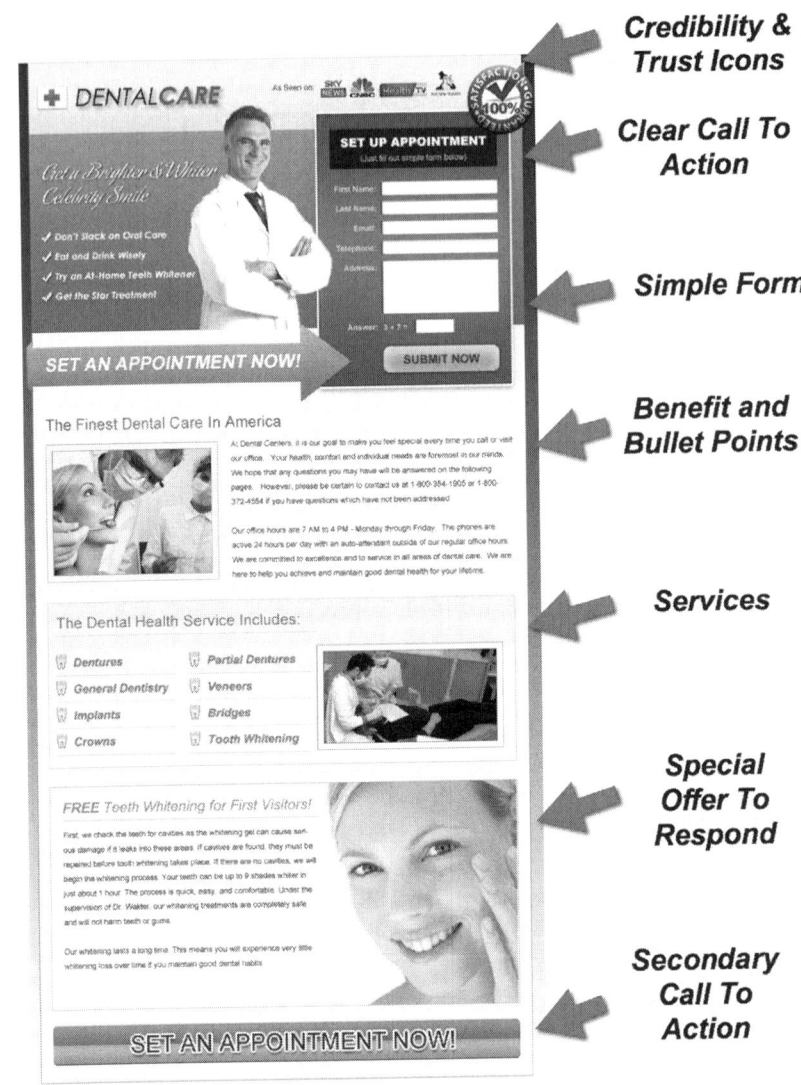

Credibility & Trust Icons

Clear Call To Action

Simple Form

Benefit and Bullet Points

Services

Special Offer To Respond

Secondary Call To Action

Example of a Landing Page

And here is another decent example of a landing page we found with some quick searches:

The image above includes the following labels:

- Easy to Find Phone Number
- Simple Web Form and Compelling Free Offer
- Embedded Google Map
- Benefit Rich Headline and Bullet Points
- Business Address
- Phone # again

Content within the image:

☎ 877-___-____

NAME

EMAIL

YOUR COMMENTS

FREE

Implants Consult &
Second Opinion

For a limited time only
(a $130 value, X-rays not included)

* Some restrictions may apply
"Mention "Free Initial Consult" when scheduling

SUBMIT

Learn More at _____

Get a Beautiful Smile with Dental Implants
from your local Southington Dentistry

Southington Dentistry offers dental implant solutions for
patients with missing teeth that look and feel much like real
ones. We know how important it is for you to smile with
confidence, knowing that your teeth look great. We use the
latest technology available to provide the best and safest
dental implants to our patients in the Plantsville area.

Dental Implants at Southington Dentistry

- **Experienced Team:** The dentists at the Southington
  Dentistry are highly experienced in effectively diagnosing
  and treating your Dental Implants needs
- **Personalized Service:** Our doctors will work with your
  develop the best individual treatment plan for you.
  Southington Dentistry is committed to the best personalized
  service and quality care.
- **Financing Available:** Southington Dentistry accepts cash,
  checks, and credit cards. We also offer a flexible No Interest
  payment plan to help you pay for treatments that your
  insurance doesn't cover.

Conveniently Located in Plantsville, CT

15-3A Cornerstone Court
Plantsville, CT 06479

☎ 877-366-7650

Another Good example of a
Landing Page for a Local Business

Let's dig a little deeper on this, because it's critically
important.

Direct Google PPC ads to <u>ad specific</u>
landing pages based on EXACTLY
what they were searching for...

One of the biggest mistakes that we see businesses
(and even other marketing agencies), make when

constructing a lead generation campaign with Google PPC ads, is not directing visitors to a product specific landing page **based on what they were searching for.**

You now know that you absolutely don't want to drive straight to your home page - and that's a good start. Plus you've created (or are going to create), a dedicated landing page for your AdWords efforts - that's even better! But... you still don't want to funnel ALL of your AdWords traffic to this one new landing page.

It's better than driving to your website's home page - without a doubt - but you can still take an added step that will ensure even higher lead conversions.

Simply put, you want to give the visitor *exactly* what they were promised in the ad.

If your ad read:

Bankruptcy **Attorney** NC
www.powerofthe**law**.net/ ▾
Meet With A **Lawyer** For Free! Save Your Property & Get A Fresh Start.

You should NOT put them on a page that talks about all of the other kinds of Law you practice. That person clicking is interested ONLY in what the ad promised and nothing more.

In an ideal world you should have different landing pages for various keyword terms. For example, if you are marketing your Law Firm with multiple specialties, you should have a different landing page for each Keyword term.

You might have a landing page specifically for **Bankruptcy Attorney.**

One specifically about **Personal Injury Law.**

Another landing page for **Divorce/Family Law.**

Yet another page for **Immigration Law.**

Don't be lazy when it comes to setting these unique pages up for your various services. If you really want to make Google Lead Generation work then you must not cut corners.

It **will** pay off if you or the agency you hire puts in this extra work.

Well-built landing pages are designed from the bottom up to convert leads and meet the prospect with exactly what they're looking for. You can take this a step further by ensuring your ad exactly matches what they'll see when they get to your Landing Page.

Here are 5 tips on how to make landing pages that will increase conversion...

In an ideal world you would have a qualified expert managing your campaign - and your Landing Page conversion strategy; working every month to make them perform. More on how to do that in a minute, but here are 5 tips to increase your results:

1. Get rid of most of your navigation – Essentially you want to funnel your visitor to where the only option for them to get off the page is have them fill out a form, call the tracking phone number on your landing page *(we use special Analytic Call Tracking numbers so that we can track inbound phone calls)* or click X and close the page.

Bear in mind this isn't to manipulate the user, but you must be able to capture relevant info quickly (e-mail, name, phone #) or else the effort of your PPC ad is squandered. Note, to appease Google you will need Privacy, Terms and Contact Us links at the bottom of the pages. Contact us and we can help you with designing your landing page so that it's compliant with Google's rules.

2. Optimize Your Contact Forms - This second tip is pretty straightforward. There is a direct correlation between the number of fields in a contact form and the conversion rate. The more information you ask for on a web form the less likely someone is to complete that form. Eliminate all fields that are nonessential and watch your conversion rate rise.

3. Have a Clear Call to Action –If you want the person who just landed on your landing page to cough up their info... then tell them to cough it up! Calls to action are one

How To Generate Leads For Your Local Business With Google AdWords

of the most overlooked components to acquiring leads, but make sure they know the benefit that is implicit to giving up their information.

4. Give Something Away For Free or Have a Good Offer - Try thinking of creative ways to generate leads because simply asking for someone's personal information won't always fill up your inbox with leads. You have to have a compelling reason why they should submit their information.

Here are a few simple ideas and examples:

- *Free Consultation* – Offer a brief consultation that requires users to fill out a contact form in order for a customer service representative to reach out and schedule an appointment.
  Free White Paper – Offer information that potential clients would find valuable, but require users to fill out a contact form in order to download it or have it emailed to them. (i.e. What You Should Know Before Getting Dental Implants).

- *Free Information Kit* – Offer to send the prospect some free information such as a DVD or information kit that explains what your business has to offer.

- *Free Webinar* – Host a webinar discussing a new product, recent research or simply an online Q&A session. There are ways to set this up in an evergreen fashion.

5. Avoid the Disconnect – If your landing page doesn't correlate to what your Google PPC ad offered, then visitors will be put off and won't do business with you. Nothing is worse than being "sold" on A but getting B instead. Don't rely on misleading PPC ads to generate business…. because it won't work well for you.

Bonus tip: Match your landing page's call to action to its headline (Free Water Test, Refinance, VA Loans, Free Teeth Whitening Consultation) so visitors truly understand what they're getting. Also, this will increase your "quality score" which will get you more clicks for cheaper.

As you may have noticed by now, we are HUGE fans of Google. We love Google's AdWords platform and the infinite amount of potential it provides to a small business to reach its audience. Google, for very good reason, has become the largest Internet search engine in the world. It offers access to an unprecedented amount of information, but it also has become the number one way for you to market your business online and pull in qualified leads.

Google's revenue growth is a testament to the fact that the AdWords Pay Per Click platform works.

Just take a look specifically at the last four years to see just how much it has grown. You might have been able to ignore the possibilities that Google brought in 2008, and maybe in 2009, but when you see their rate of growth in recent years, you have to realize that Google is not going anywhere anytime soon.

How To Generate Leads For Your Local Business With Google AdWords

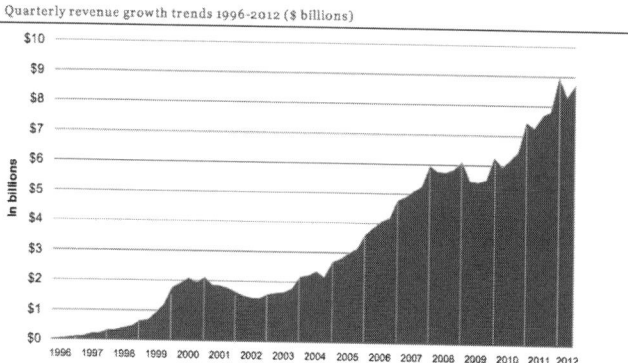

Quarterly revenue growth trends 1996-2012 ($ billions)

Google's Revenue Growth Trend
from 1996 - 2012

They are only going to get bigger and better at what they do by implementing new advancements to AdWords. In fact, Google's stock price just took a large spike and it is attributed to Mobile Ads. Your prospects and customers have gone Mobile and are doing search for local businesses like yours - so this will only continue.

In this day and age, if you're not on Google, you're being left behind. Get there and solidify your position before your competition does. Your length of time as an advertiser also affects your quality score and cost per click. If you've been a good advertiser for longer than your competitors than you're at a slight advantage - so there's no better time to get started than NOW!

8. Here's What To Do Next...

Our sincere hope is that we've shown you the possibilities that Google AdWords holds in driving qualified leads to your business. We hope that you've learned some ways that Google AdWords can help grow your business and even further, we hope that you've learned some things you should absolutely look for if you're considering hiring anyone to manage Google AdWords Campaigns for your business.

Here are a few options that you have as far as we see it:

The 'Don't Do Anything' option: We seriously hope that you don't choose this path. Unless your average ticket price is just so low it wouldn't make sense to invest in attracting new customers via Google AdWords then we think you'd be passing up on a big opportunity.

The 'Do it Yourself' Option: If you are going to tackle Google AdWords on your own we recommend following Perry Marshall and getting his **_Ultimate Guide To Google AdWords_** as that will be a great next step to learn the mechanics of setting up campaigns from a **master**.

**The 'Hire an Expert' Option**: Finally, if you believe in focusing on the management and growth of your business as your chief roll, and you'd like a team of experts to take over your Google AdWords campaign management then this option is for you. Whether you have tried Google AdWords before and didn't have success or you've never tried it before but see the value in having experts manage your account, then this is the best option for you.

If you'd like, we can schedule a _**100% Free consultation to answer any questions you have**_ and see what a Google AdWords campaign may look like for your business. You can claim that by _**clicking here**_.

Even further, if you currently have someone in house or an outside agency managing your campaign we can complete an account audit for you 100% Free as well.

Most businesses that have tried to manage Google AdWords themselves that failed, or hired another company that didn't deliver, were probably missing these seemingly small but important things. Its also possible they didn't have enough experience to know the small, subtle campaign tweaks that can turn a losing campaign into a 10x winner... we do, and are happy to talk with you about them.

To claim this Free consultation please Click Here

We'd be happy to help in any way that we can.

(Please note that we are very busy and will schedule your consultation as soon as we can).

One Last Thing...

Firstly, we would like to say "Thank You" for reading this book and we hope that you found value here. We know that your time and attention are incredibly valuable and we thank you for yours.

Now that you have arrived at the end of our book, if you are reading this on a Kindle enabled device, Amazon will give you the opportunity to rate this book, leave a review, and share your thoughts on Facebook and Twitter. (Even if you read the physical version you can help with this too).

We hope that you've gotten a lot of value from this book and enjoyed reading it as much as we've enjoyed putting it together.

If so, then we would truly appreciate it if you could take just 30 seconds to leave a positive rating, a quick review, and share your thoughts with your friends on social media.

We'll be extremely grateful and would love to see what you have to say!

Sincerely,
Kyle Battis & Mike Purvis

What People Are Saying...

"If you're serious about your personal success Kyle will be your greatest asset."

-Jonathon Olla

"The ability to work exclusively with these guys and dominate your market is invaluable."

-Jeremiah Poljacik
Real Estate Marketing Company

"I have had my share with digital marketing companies and had nothing but slow responses and large bills, nothing but headaches. That changed when I started working with Kyle and Mike. If you're looking for a company to give your company a quick jump start then Kyle is your man and NH Strategic Marketing is your company...."

- Captain 'Bob' Hamilton

"The Best Speaker we have ever had..."

-Tammy Hastings
Center for Women's Business Advancement
Southern New Hampshire University

9. About The Authors

Kyle Battis

Kyle is an Amazon.com #1 Best Seller of "***The Formula – How To Grow Your Business with Smart Online & Mobile Marketing***." Kyle is a Local Marketing expert specializing in helping small business owners siphon qualified leads from the Internet.

Mike Purvis

Mike is Google AdWords Certified, and has designed, managed and honed campaigns for 5 million dollar plus companies. Mike's campaigns have resulted in profitable traffic in difficult markets where others had failed.

Sources:

- Google Investor Relations
- The War On Free Clicks
- Google Economic Impact Report
- AdWords Blog
- Breaking Down Google's 2011 Revenue
- Specific Media
- Accurcast

Printed in Great Britain
by Amazon.co.uk, Ltd.,
Marston Gate.